Black Women Who Have Made a Difference

Black Women Who Have Made a Difference

Minnie L. Ransom, Ed.D.

Table of Contents

Dedicated to Sharonda, Kaliah, Siobhan, Kaliese, Mui, Chloe,
and all girls and women in the world.

Introduction

Respect Yourself and Others
By: Dr. Minnie Ransom

Show respect for yourself, others, and their differences.

You never know the consequences.

Have hope for the future which is essential.

Always living up to your full potential.

Be a part of change for the better:

Many dreams potentially not to shatter.

Being true to yourself is what really matters.

Accept defeat with grace and know,

That everything presents a lesson to grow.

Never give up even when doors are closed.

Someday your blessings will overflow.

You may be treated wrong but stand for what is right.

In the end it will be worth the fight.

Slang, vulgar, and obscene language is not a part of your vocabulary.

You are smart and can use many other words from the dictionary.

Pull up those pants: Be proud, not shy.

Represent the proud people you are, holding your head high.

Walk tall as if your heads were being pulled to the sky.

Sit up in your chair.

There is no time to spare.

Head down, drifting off will not get you there.

Sit at the front of the class, sitting in the back has long passed.

Focus! Be in the present; One place and not head is in another.

Listen! Really listen; Take everything all in.

Participate. Not distracting or being distracted by others.

Learning is not a sin! Learning starts from within.

Learn all that is presented to you from class beginning to end.

Being called Nerd, Teacher's Pet, Show-Off, or even a Geek.

Do not let those make you weak.

When they say words trying to make you turn within and hurt yourself,

Disregard those evil words spewed seeking to put themselves on a shelf.

Leave those fears and negativities behind you.

Of which I am sure there are a few.

Even when you are accused of trying to be more than who you are.

You will not let that stop you from being a star.

When asked if you think you are better than the rest,

You know for you what is best.

All of this is not a sheer coincidence.

Draw strength from God and from within to help you with endurance.

They will try to snuff out your light burning ever so bright.

May this possibly be the one way to show their might?

Could it be the only way to make their light begin to flicker?

They may think that they are slicker.

Being all that you can be is demonstrating your true presence!

To not show your brilliance is to be of non-existence!

Phillis Wheatley (1753-1784)

During 1761 in the Boston harbor,

A little slave girl was discovered buried in the body of a vessel.

She was likely 6 to 8 years old and a foreigner.

She was sold to a wealthy merchant tailor for his wife,

Who had compassion for her which would relieve the little girl's strife.

She was treated as a daughter and assigned chores,

Relative to a position of any lady, mine, or yours'.

She was described as "my Phillis".

Phillis was instructed to read and write.

By the Wheatley's children of birth right.

Phillis was a quick study.

She learned the English language within eighteen months,

She had learned so well that she could read anything quite blunt.

It was clear that her intelligence had been seen rarely.

She even became proficient in Latin fearlessly.

At the age of 14 she began to write poetry.

Before long, the news of her gifts captured attraction,

Of distinguished Bostonians' attention,

Some of which had human consideration.

In 1770 Phillis wrote her first published poem,

"On the Death of the Rev. Mr. George Whitegield".

The poem came to the attention of the Countess of Huntington in England.

Three years later Phillis was sent to England for health reasons,

The Countess introduced her to the Lord Mayor and other members of nobility.

Phillis impressed them so much that before she left,

The Countess had arranged to have a volume of her poems published.

In 1773, the first book of poems of various subjects on religion and moral,

By an American Black woman off the press was relinquished.

A forward was signed by eighteen prominent Massachusetts men,

Including the wealthy merchant John Hancock and the governor of the colony.

Proving her authorship and talents that were indeed only hers awesomely.

That little girl, Phillis Wheatley who arrived in the belly of a ship,

Became a pioneer in literary history, a poetess of the American Revolution,

And the first Black female poetess in the United States

Her mistress died in 1774 and her master died in 1778 leaving her a free person.

Which soon became a burden.

She became an instant slave of hard times, sadness, and a life of poverty.

Until the Revolutionary War change her li fe from being a bondwoman.

One month after the master's death, she married John Peters,

Who was not a good provider and Phillis' life was now perplex.

She found herself being forced to work as a servant, her life to protect.

Her life now was certainly not vibrant.

She had two children which died soon after birth.

Her health started to fail.

During this time, she wrote a long poem,

"Liberty and Peace" on Dec. 5, 1784 just before she and her

Third child died within hours of each other.

Phillis Wheatley

https://www.loc.gov/item/2002712199/

Bessie Smith (1894-1937)

Born into poverty in Chattanooga, Tennessee,

One of seven children you see.

She was orphaned at an early age,

Raised by her older sister which turned the page.

She started earning a living by singing on the streets.

It could help them to eat.

She joined a traveling show in 1912.

She was born not to fail.

She was known as the "Queen and Empress of the Blues".

With Columbia Record Company teetering on the brink of bankruptcy,

Her talents were successfully used nationally.

After signing her contract, she was credited with averting that lite fuse.

She sold as many as 100,000 records in a week,

During a difficult time in the record industry.

At the peak of her career displayed her talent,

To Blacks and Whites as an actress recording 160 songs.

In 1933, her career faltered when the blues craze began to fade.

On the way to Memphis her car collided with a parked panel truck.

It flipped over and from us she was plucked.

Her arm was nearly severed and had to be amputated.

She died after that horrible accident and for more than 30 years,

A marker on her grave waited.

Even though, her talents tremendously influenced great singers

Young and old.

Billie Holiday and Mahalia Jackson to name two,

There are plenty others, and everyone knows it is true.

At least a marker should have been added if the truth would to be told.

Not until two locals paying one half each of the marker sold,

Set a wrong right with their hearts of gold.

Frances Ellen W. Harper (1825-1911)

Frances was born of free parents in Baltimore, Maryland.

After her parents died when she was at the age of three,

She was an orphan.

She was sent to live with an outspoken uncle, a reverend,

Abolitionist, practicing self-taught medicine,

Organized a black literary society and established his own school.

Watkins Academy for Negro Youth established in 1820.

Frances learned from his activism until she was thirteen years old.

When children were typically expected to join the workforce,

We are told.

At age 13, she went to work as a domesticated.

Using the family library there, continued to be educated.

On her own studying in which she was dedicated.

As a teen began writing poetry.

With pen and paper, they told a story.

Her collection of verse and style were published in 1845.

She moved to Pennsylvania in the1850's to teach school.

While there she was drawn into the cause of anti-slavery.

The sheer act undeniably displayed her bravery.

First, with her pen and later, speaking up for those,

Whose voices were suppressed and made weaker,

She became one of the country's most eloquent speakers.

By age twenty-one, Harper wrote her first small volume of poetry.

Referred to by a newspaperwoman as the "Bronze Muse".

She was the first Black American to publish a short story.

She was the second to publish a novel.

Traveling across the United States and Canada as a lecturer,

Never known to grovel.

She was hired as a traveling lecturer for various organizations.

Speaking on antislavery, illustrating her bravery.

Committed to the struggle for women's rights,

She won over even more of the Whites.

She started including her observations from her travels.

Her writings began to unravel the inequities in published novels.

Short stories, and poetry focusing on issues of racism,

Feminism and classism,

Woven deeply within the American system.

She had alliances with prominent women's rights activists,

Supporting the fifteenth amendment,

Granting African American men, the right to vote,

Being the right thing they wanted to promote,

Along with Frederick Douglass and many others,

They wanted equal rights for their sisters and brothers.

She helped to form the American Woman Suffrage Association.

It facilitated better understanding the movement and education.

She spent the rest of her career working for the pursuit of equal rights,

Job opportunities, and education for African American women's plight.

Black women were facing the double problem of racism and sexism,

At the same time, because of the color of their skin they had to fight.

Her topics varied and full of voice unconstrained,

Feelings and emotional fortitude.

She indeed showed a lot of attitude.

She felt that former slave owners and newly freed slaves' lives,

Were connected as phrases and sentences, oceans, and waves.

One could not succeed at the expense of the other.

MRS. FRANCIS E. W. HARPER.

Harriet Ross Tubman (1820-1913)

Harriet Tubman was born a slave approximately in 1820;

Recordings for Blacks, there were not many.

From an early age Harriet was brutalized and forced;

To perform hard labor by her masters but she never failed.

It toughened her body that would later demonstrate to her avail;

In later years giving her unrelenting stamina that served her well.

Being stuck in her head with a two-pound weight,

Fracturing her skull at the age of thirteen;

This amazing woman was still braver than anyone had ever seen.

The injury caused her to have dizziness and uncontrollable sleeping spells.

For the rest of her life, she couldn't be easily awaken even by bells.

During these times God would give her visions that served her well.

Unsure of her faith after her master died to freedom she escaped.

Although being free, she wasn't just satisfied with her own autonomy;

Remaining true to the way her life was shaped.

Having a strong belief, faith in God, and the right to liberty,

She wasn't satisfied with her people being in day to day misery.

Risking her own life making 19 dangerous trips;

Into the deep-rooted intolerant South,

Avoiding brutal punishment including the whips;

Unselfishly guiding over 300 slaves to freedom;

Safely making the dream of freedom a reality.

For freedom from slavery and new found liberty desired,

Escaping to the North was required.

When Harriet could not be guided by the North Star;

Using the moss growing on the North side of trees,

She used to avoid a snare.

Guiding her Northward on foggy and cloudy nights;

Her system would not squander and was always very concise.

Harriet was one of the greatest and bravest

Underground Railroad conductors;

Even with a $40,000 reward for her capture and small in structure.

Because it was dangerous for anyone to help "property" to escape;

Her own brother overcome by fear,

Turned back while escaping with her near.

From then on no one else ever turned back on her again. She simply would not

allow it; She would command;

"You'll be free or you will die," once signed on you were to withstand.

She was known to say,

"I never ran my train off the track and I never lost a passenger."

During the Civil War, Harriet served as a scout, spy, and nurse for the Union

Army.

She led the Union Army on a raid which resulted in that journey;

In the year 1863 freed slaves of 750.

Later after her dedicated service, she applied for military pension.

Forced to live in poverty for 30 years her plight went without attention.

Finally, after congress passed a private bill in 1897;

She was granted $20. a month which she used for a driven passion.

She established the Harriet Tubman Home;

For deprived aged Blacks forgotten and left all alone.

Receiving financial aid from Great Britain and Canada,

She was able to continue her fight at home.

Queen Victoria sent her expensive gifts;

Invitations to visit her in Britain among the lists.

She lived to be 93 years old;

Buried in Ohio with military honors.

Harriet was known as "Moses of Her People".

Her faith in God and an unfailing desire to help others;

Caused her to manage to escape her would-be captors.

Thousands of Blacks and Whites gathered to give her tributes.

In the words of Booker T. Washington,

"She brought the two races together

Making it possible for the White race,

To place a higher value on the Black race,"

As being one of her greatest attributes.

Ida B. Wells Barnett (1862-1931)

Ida B. Wells was born in Holly Spring, Mississippi.

She was orphaned at the age of fourteen.

Despite her adversity,

Attended Rust College and Fisk University.

Ida was a writer, teacher, lecturer,

Most courageous Black woman journalist.

Co-founder of the NAACP and was also a Social Worker and an activist.

She taught in segregated public schools until she was discharged,

For writing a controversial article to tell in those days was hard.

When Black businessmen were being lynched for defending,

Their own property she wrote an editorial identifying,

And the murderers brought to justice she was demanding.

All the equipment and articles in the printing office,

Were destroyed but did not stop her from fighting unfair practice of lawless.

Later she discredited the mythology that Black men were being lynched,

Because they raped White women, making their unfair justice cinched.

Being strong-willed and spirited,

Refused when asked to leave the "White"

Section of the train because it was not merited.

She was forcefully removed by 3 conductors,

Who were determined to be the means of her destructors.

She sued and won $500 in damages that were later overturned,

Such a victory as that, her race could not be earned.

In 1895 she married Ferdinard Barnett.

As an attorney he helped her to expose in their newspaper,

Injustice perpetrated against Blacks without regret.

When the townspeople were too afraid to go along,

To protest the reinstatement of the sheriff who was permitting murders,

She was known to simply go on her own.

Pleading for more than a day and won.

She was instrumental in ending the lynching in Illinois.

Best known as the champion of the turn-of-the-century, Anti-lynching crusader
of our ancestry.

Cited as one of the 25 outstanding women in Chicago's history,

She did what she felt was best, no matter who it may annoy.

IDA B. WELLS.

Mary McLeod Bethune (1875-1955)

Mary Mcleod Bethune was born to slave parents,

On this side of slavery in Mayesville, South Carolina.

As a child she always had a strong desire for knowledge,

Of which for Blacks was being held in hostage.

There were no schools for her in Mayesville until age 11.

This fact was not stopping her from walking five miles daily,

For the desired education that had been in her aroused.

After graduation she won a small scholarship,

From a white woman in Denver, Colorado.

Who wanted to help one Black child attain more education.

Mary with admiration and appreciation,

Went on to graduate from Scotia Seminary in Concord,

North Carolina in 1893.

She felt that her opportunities to learn

Brought with it a certain responsibility,

Of sharing her knowledge with others of her race.

She wanted to go to Africa as a missionary,

Being too young, the Mission Board felt was what she was dealt.

Instead, she founded her school for girls in 1904,

With a mere $1.50, five girls, packing crates,

salvaged goods from the dumps, in a rented cabin in Florida,

Without any additional help financial or

Otherwise and nothing from a store.

The school grew and later, it became a four-year college accredited,

That later merged with Cookman Institute

With a student body of six hundred,

32 faculty members, and an $800,000 campus free of debt!

She also held many government positions,

Appointed to positions in the White House

By President Hoover and President Truman.

She was also a consultant to the presidents, of great race relationships.

The first black woman to establish a school in the United States.

She received many awards in London,

Including being received by lords and ladies there.

Blessed also by the Pope in Rome.

Mary McLeod Bethune left a legacy to her people,

The philosophy of living and serving would be,

Inspirational to those who share her vision of world peace.

Mary McLeod Bethune's Last Will and Testament

If I have a legacy to leave my people, it is,

My philosophy of living and serving.

Here, Then, is My Legacy…

I leave you love; Love builds.

It is positive and helpful.

I leave you hope. Yesterday, our ancestors

Endured the degradation of slavery, yet they

Retained their dignity.

I leave you the challenge of developing,

confidence in one another. This kind of

confidence will aid the economic rise of

the race by bringing together the pennies,

and dollars of our people and ploughing them,

into useful channels.

I leave you thirst for education. Knowledge

Is the prime need of the hour.

I leave you a respect for the uses of power,

Power, Intelligently directed, can lead to more freedom.

I leave you faith. Faith in God is the greatest power,

But great, too, is faith in oneself.

I leave you racial dignity.

I want Negroes to maintain their human dignity at all costs.

I leave you a desire to live harmoniously,

With your fellow man.

I leave you, finally, a responsibility to our, Young people.

The world around us really belongs,

to youth for will take over its future management.

Mary McLeod Bethune

MARY McLEOD BETHUNE
1875 1955
Let her works praise her

OWI-14831-E

Sojourner Truth (1797-1883)

Sojourner Truth was born Isabella Baumfree,

In 1797 near Kingston, New York.

She was sold from master to master.

While with one master she was forced to marry,

Bearing five children with an older slave,

Heartlessly several were sold off.

She escaped in 1827 and took refuge,

With a Quaker family whose name she took.

Along with their assistance won a lawsuit,

And one son returned to her.

Now freed with the New York State,

Emancipation Act in 1828,

Sojourner was one of the best renowned,

American abolitionists around.

She was the first Black female speechmaker,

To speak out against slavery being their messenger.

She was an effective speaker,

With a voice that demanded attention.

A stature that commanded respect.

She quickly put to rest,

The myth that women were the weaker sex.

She publicly proved that she was not a man.

In a way that they all could understand.

She was not disguised as a woman was her demand.

Only that she and other women work just as hard as any man.

Women did not receive the same privileges,

Even though that was their wishes.

She could not read or write.

Still, she became a preacher, traveling across the country,

Lecturing on abolition and the rights of the "lesser sex".

She said that God gave her the name "Sojourner",

When she had asked for a new name.

She was showing people their sins,

Being a sign unto them from within.

He also gave her "Truth",

Because she was to declare,

The truth unto the People,

A pilgrim of freedom.

A passionate women's rights activist,

She served as a nurse, raised money,

For soldiers' gifts, and helped to resettle,

Many slaves who fled from the South for a life better.

She was received at the White House in her prime,

By President Lincoln and was a legend of her time.

Sojourner embraced all human plights,

That were being infringed upon and denied their rights!

If de fust woman God ever made was strong enough to turn de world upside down all alone, dese women all togedder ought to be able to turn it back and get it right side up again.—*Sojourner Truth.*

Marian Anderson (1903-1993)

Marian was born in Philadelphia, PA; Her mother was a domestic.

Father sold coal and ice but well respected.

Showing at an early age the talent for singing, she supplemented.

Her parents' income by singing in church concerts that were presented.

In high school her teachers recognized her talents

And urged her to take classes.

She auditioned for famed voice tutors

And was accepted as a talented pupil being unsurpassed.

Her first year's tuition was paid for at church

With collections of nickels and dimes,

That could go a long way during those times.

She was once passed over time after time while waiting in line

All day determined to enter the music school

Which was of the contrary for the time.

Finally, when no one else entered the line,

was rudely asked what she wanted was the query.

Later she won a scholarship but like other Blacks of the era,

Were discriminated against by those who thought they were superior.

Forced to seek fame and fortune where her talents would be appreciated,

In Europe, she was proven to be the greatest.

Desperate to make a concert appearance, $500 she paid a concertmaster,

To accompany her to Berlin where the audience was entranced.

They had witnessed a part of history

To be a particularly important chapter,

Her flawless control of her vocal of three octaves

And ability to sing in nine different languages,

Proved to all under all circumstances she was far beyond the averages.

No matter the race her abilities were far in advanced.

The Berlin concert began a frantic concert pace,

Unknown by any race.

Becoming the world's most popular, highest paid, and talented,

Marian in her own way in dignity and grace

Away from her country rose above racism.

Nevertheless, the daughters of the American Revolution,

A concert performance in Washington D.C. they denied.

Constitutional rights and equal opportunities denied was the decision.

In her great wisdom Eleanor Roosevelt resigned her membership.

First Lady Roosevelt invited Marian to perform in an outdoor concert,

One of which finally in America would be remembered.

History worthy in our day.

At the Lincoln Memorial on Easter Sunday,

Her talents to 75,000 people she could articulate

And would not be deprived.

Marian was later known to have the contralto voice of the century.

To help others who would come after her,

Anderson established an award,

In her name to help struggling singers.

She had a desire to sing at the Metropolitan Opera House,

Where no Black had ever sang.

Eventually to let her voice echo through the building was her opportunity.

It was an outstanding performance bringing more popularity.

As a result of those who had preceded her,

She earned more awards than them all.

After her final concert in New York City at the Carnegie Hall,

She retired in Connecticut with her husband.

She was 90 years old when she died.

There were no barriers she did not overcome that she had tried.

Throughout her life she showed grace and dignity,

Staying true to her dream to prove her talents she did not flee.

Throughout all the racism and hatred of being talented and Black

She was always willing to give back.

There are many persons ready to do what is right because in their hearts they know it is right. But they hesitate, waiting for the other fellow to make the first move, and he, waits for you. The minute a person whose word means a great deal dares to take the open-hearted and courageous way; many others follow. Not everyone can be turned aside from meanness and hatred, but the great majority of Americans is heading in that direction. I have a great belief in the future of my people and my country.
– Marian Anderson

It is easy to look back, self-indulgently, feeling pleasantly sorry for oneself and saying I didn't have this and I didn't have that. But it is only the grown woman regretting the hardships of a little girl who never thought they were hardships at all. She had the things that really mattered.
– Marian Anderson, 1956

As long as you keep a person down, some part of you has to be down there to hold him down, so it means you cannot soar as you otherwise might.
– Marian Anderson

You lose a lot of time, hating people.
-- Marian Anderson, 1965

Mary Eliza Mahoney,
R.N. (1845-1926)

Mary was born in Roxbury, Massachusetts, the oldest child of three.

Of her life before she enrolled in nursing school extraordinarily little was to see.

She enrolled in nursing school in 1878 on March 26.

Before becoming a student, she was employed,

At the hospital as a maid-of all-work that she enjoyed.

After she enrolled, nurses' training was lengthened,

Academic standards became more rigorous.

She would not let that discourage her from being disciplined.

Of the 18 students who began the program, nine continued,

Only four including Mary received their coveted diploma.

Despite the hospital's strict requirements,

She conquered them all with such fortitude and charisma.

Mary withstood the pressure and maintained,

An exceptionally good record despite the rigid trends of discrimination.

Her excellence eventually paved the way,

She never wanted the color of skin to be a nurse cause someone delay,

Her desire was for others like her who wanted to be a nurse,

Their skin color should not be held as a curse.

She felt that those wanting to be a nurse,

Should not be held back because of their color.

Those who knew her described her as being interesting,

Possessing an unusual personality, and very charming.

She worked as a private-duty nurse for the best families in Boston,

Her clients praised her for her calm efficiency.

She participated with enthusiasm in her nurse's association.

The second year of the National Association of

Colored Graduate Nurses she delivered the welcome address.

At which time she was elected the chaplain and given life membership.

She was a fervent supporter of women's suffrage.

She knew unjustified discrimination firsthand and being held at bondage.

She was one of the first Black women in Boston to register to vote.

Mary died of cancer at the New England Hospital

For Women and Children at the age of 81 in 1926.

The National Association of Colored Graduate Nurses

Established the Mary Mahoney Award in 1936.

The Mary Mahoney Award is now given in her honor,

For outstanding contributions to intergroup relation,

By the American Nurse Association.

Mary Edmona Lewis (1846-1890)

Mary was born in Greenhigh, Ohio in 1846.

Her father was a freed Negro and a gentleman's servant.

Her mother was a Chippewa Indian. Her parents died when she was young,

It is not known who raise her beyond.

She attended Oberlin College in Ohio.

She studied Latin and Greek. The school did not offer art,

She decided there, however that she wanted to be a sculptress from the start.

During the fall term of her fourth year, her college days came to and end.

She moved to Boston. It seemed that she just could not win.

In the Boston's City Hall square,

She first studied the statue of Benjamin Franklin,

With renewed interest of being a sculptress she did declare.

She knew that she too could make a "stone man".

She became obsessed to prove to the world her worth.

She was introduced to Brackett, a leading sculptor,

Who immediately realized her talent that was cultivated from birth.

Her medallion of John Brown, an abolitionist, was to be an excellent piece.

Her first piece, critics declared, would be a masterpiece.

As an excellent piece, she was well on her way.

She then created the bust of Colonel Robert Gould Shaw.

A socially prominent White commander of Massachusetts'

First Negro regiment attracted wide attention.

To add to her sculptured addition.

It established Mary as the first Black American sculptress.

She later received the support of a well-known family named Story,

In Boston who helped to sell her sculptures, so she needed not to worry.

And encouraged her to study in Italy.

In 1865, she went to Rome to master her skills actively.

She worked in marble and was noted for her exacting mastery.

Great artist came to examine and praise her work of artistry,

She was befriended by famous artists and patronized by royalty.

She received her greatest recognition abroad.

At home she could not even receive an applaud.

She returned to the United States in 1876 and was then the only,

Black artist to exhibit in Philadelphia's Centennial Exposition.

Her bust of poet; Henry Wadsworth Longfellow can be seen,

In the Widener library of Harvard University.

In 1870 she created a bust of Abraham Lincoln seen,

In the California Municipal Library in San Jose, California.

Dr. Susan McKinney Steward (1848-1918)

Susan Smith was born in Brooklyn, New York.

She was the first to enter the medical profession

And to gain recognizable success.

Even after being confronted with two barriers,

There was no one to help; She let her strength be her carrier.

Being a woman and Black

Highly motivated and determined,

She overcame both and graduated.

Barriers she overcame through all the hatred.

Graduating from the New York Medical School for Women and Children,

Valedictorian of her class proved her greatness.

She refused to let anything hold her back.

The next year she married William G. McKinney,

Becoming the mother of two children, a daughter and son.

She did her post graduate work at Long Island College Hospital,

Further was distinguished as being the only female in her class.

She practiced homeopathy in the hospital

And dispensary making a clear contrast.

Her practice grew so large that it had to be relocated creating a better path,

For later renaming it the Memorial Hospital for Women and Children.

She had a successful private practice in Brooklyn for more than 20 years,

And eventually opened a second office in Manhattan among her peers.

After her husband's death, she became an organist and choirmaster,

A board member for aged Colored People was another

Call she had to answer.

Being an avid of history and progress of women in medicine,

Later, becoming the founder of

Women's Royal Union of New York and Brooklyn.

Her concern and feelings for her people and women were genuine.

She became an active member of the Kings Country Homeopathic Society.

Later on she married an army chaplain and instructor

At Wilberforce University.

Shortly thereafter she left Brooklyn

And made her home in Wilberforce, Ohio.

She continued her passion of helping others

And practiced medicine for many years.

Madame C.J. Walker (1867-1919)

Madame C.J. Walker was born Sarah Breedlove

On December 23, 1867 in Delta, Louisiana to ex-slave parents of.

She lost both her parents at the age of six.

She was raised by a married sister.

She became Mrs. McWilliams at the age of 14 and had one daughter.

By the age of 20 she was a widow. No other children did she have as she grew

older. In 1887 she moved to St. Louis where she took in washing.

She educated herself by attending night school.

For 18 years earning $1.50 a day doing work that was back breaking.

A strong desire to get relief from this work so cruel.

Soon she made an investment of one day's work to do an experiment.

She mixed one concoction after another in her washtub becoming weaken,

Her knuckles were sour and her back felt as if it was nearly broken.

Hairdressing formula for Black women's hair was her acknowledgement.

In 1905 she invented and patented a straightening comb

For Black women to use with her hairdressing.

It turned out to be another one of her blessings.

In 1906 she married Charles Joseph Walker,

A newspaperman and was known thereafter as Madame C.J. Walker.

Madame C.J. Walker would travel to demonstrate her technique,

Which became known as the Madame C.J. Walker method.

Her method was not known in the day and unique.

At first, the Walker method was ridiculed by Black and Whites.

She continued to demonstrate her method with the concept in her head molded.

After one year she was able to open an office,

And manufacturing headquarters in Denver.

Madame Walker was a survivor.

She traveled for two years alone,

Having stamina and the will to succeed unknown.

She had a vision that was extraordinarily strong.

Demonstrating her technique from door to door.

Never to be poor again she swore.

She was so successful in her personal selling and mail orders,

That she soon opened a second office in Philadelphia.

She was on her way and nothing could stop her.

In 1908 the second office was managed by her daughter.

Her husband assisted in the business at first, not being able to stay the course,

Soon they divorced.

Later both offices were consolidated in Indianapolis,

Indiana where a plant was built.

By 1919 the company stretched an entire city block.

This would be the company's organization and foundational rock.

Provided employment for over three thousand people.

Giving back and helping others she was extremely noble.

Stressing cleanliness and loveliness her hair, scalp, and beauty culturists

Became familiar throughout the United States and the Caribbean.

Her agents were required to sign contracts binding them to a regiment,

Of hygienic demanded by Madame C.J. Walker for advertisement,

Eventually it came to be incorporated into the state cosmetology laws.

Madame C.J. Walker became one of the best-known Blacks in this country and

Europe.

She became America's first Black millionaire businesswoman.

She was an exceedingly kind and generous benefactress,

Of the Black community donating to NAACP, the YMCA,

Homes for the aged, sponsoring Black artists and writers,

Awarding scholarships to young women at Tuskegee

And Palmer Memorial Institutes, sponsoring Mary McLeod Bethune,

Ida B. Wells, and donating $100,000 toward construction,

In West Africa an academy to help girls was the assumption.

To continue her goodwill and charitable freewill, she made the declaration,

To also provided in her will that two-thirds of her profits from her business,

Be allotted to charitable organizations.

At her death on May 25, 1919,

Her empire was more than one million dollars and real estate,

Holdings of which one was a 30- room mansion, her will would mandate.

It to be left to her daughter In New York.

Bessie Coleman (1893-1926)

Bessie was born in 1893 in Atlanta, Texas She was the 12th of 13 children.

Her mother could not read or write,

But managed to get books from a traveling wagon that came each year twice;

Bessie would read to the rest of the family.

She had a desire to learn and better her condition.

She finished high school and wanted to go to an academic institution,

Her mother could not afford to send her.

Bessie was determined that her drive to learn it would not deter.

Her mother allowed her to keep her earnings from washing and ironing,

To attend Langston Industrial College with the money she would be keeping.

Her money only lasted one semester. She had to figure out where to go.

She went to live with her older brother in Chicago.

Attended beauty school and worked as a manicurist,

At the White Sox Barber Shop. She continued to be an avid reader.

She soon began to devour any and everything on flying.

By the end of World War 1 she had made a firm decision to fly.

Her ques to obtain flying instruction was met with blatant prejudice.

This minor setback caused Bessie to face temporary anxiousness.

For her race and being a woman denied, she met both obstacles' head on.

She went to the editor and publisher of the Chicago Weekly Defender for assistance.

She would not let the obstacles conceal her potential and competence.

After extensive research, he advised her to study French and to go to France,

They were more liberal. She was willing to take the chance.

With the money she had earned being a manicurist and working at a chili parlor,

She made two trips to Europe studying,

Under the best European flyers, including the chief pilot,

For the Germany's Fokker Aircraft Company knowledge, she was absorbing.

She received her pilot's license,

From Federation Aeronautique Internationale in France.

When she returned from Europe the second time in 1922,

She returned as the only Black female pilot in the entire world.

Another dream of Bessie's was to start a flying school,

To teach other Blacks to fly. Money being a problem,

She started doing flying exhibitions to raise money for her school.

In between exhibitions she gave lectures,

On aviation in movie houses and churches.

Once in her home state she refused to do an exhibition,

Unless Blacks could use the same entrance as Whites.

They were permitted to enter through the same entrance,

But were seated in a different section.

She had her first accident while doing an advertisement,

For Firestone Rubber Company in 1924.

When asked to do an exhibition for the Jacksonville,

Florida Negro Welfare League after opening her school,

Turned out to not be very cool,

She had a fatal accident on April 30, 1926.

On the 10th anniversary of her death,

The Chicago Weekly Defender presented the most eloquently commented,

Statement on her life and death, mentioning that others of her race were,

Encouraged to carry on in the field of aviation and that whatever is accomplished,

By her race in the field of aviation will be a memorial to her.

Every year on Memorial Day,

Pilots fly over her grave and in her honor drop flowers her way.

Patricia Roberts Harris (1924-1985)

Patricia was born on May 31, 1924 in Mattoon, IL.

She graduated *summa cum laude* from Howard in 1945 with a B.A. degree.

She did her postgraduate work at the University of Chicago,

And at American University in 1949.

Demonstrating her brilliance of the time.

She worked as Assistant Director of American Council on Human Rights

In keeping to her interest, even while she was a student at Howard,

She was interested in politics to take it to new heights.

While at Howard she met William Beasley Harris a member of,

Howard law faculty who became her husband.

She earned her degree with honors from George Washington University in 1960,

And graduated number one out of her class of 94, no less than what she had

visioned. As an adult her interest led her to a career,

That brought her to the attention of political leaders, worthy to adhere.

Her first position with the U.S. government was as an attorney in the appeal,

And research section of criminal division of the Department of Justice in 1960.

Where friends with the attorney general, Robert Kennedy she became.

President, John F. Kennedy appointed her co-chairman,

Of the National Women's Committee for Civil Rights in 1963.

In 1964, Patricia Harris was elected a delegate to Democratic National

Convention From the District of Columbia.

She was acknowledged to practice before the U.S. Supreme Court.

Before returning to Howard, she worked briefly for the Department of Justice;

As a law lecturer at Howard's law school and dean of students associate.

She was promoted to full professorship in 1960 and named,

Dean of Howard University's School of Law.

She worked in Lyndon Johnson's campaign at the 1964 Democratic Convention.

President Johnson appointed her Ambassador to Luxembourg from 1965 to

1967. Of the Democratic National Committee in 1973, She would take charge.

She was appointed chairman of the credential committee and member at large.

At the Senate confirmation committee to approve her cabinet appointment,

One senator suggested that such a position would make her ill qualified,

To serve the underclass, of her statue, he felt she was not certified.

Patricia reminded him that she was one of them,

A daughter of a dining-car worker and a Black woman unable to buy,

In parts of the District of Columbia a house for her race was not recognized.

President Jimmy Carter appointed her to two cabinet level posts,

During his administration she proved her worth without boast.

In 1982 she was appointed a full-time professor,

At George Washington National Law Center where-

She served until her death on March 23, 1985.

Patricia never forgot her roots.

She would help one to look beyond the suits.

Patricia represents two first- She was the first Black woman,

To serve in a president's cabinet and the first Black to serve,

As secretary of Health and Human Service, making her mark in Congress.

Shirley A. Chisholm (1924-2005)

Shirley Chisholm was born in Brooklyn, New York on Nov. 30, 1924.

Her parents were from the West Indies. She was a daughter, one of four.

Her father was an unskilled worker and her mother a seamstress and domestic.

The parent's most important goal was to be sure that their girls were educated.

Shirley attended a Brooklyn girls' high school and then entered Brooklyn

College, to earn her B/A. in sociology with *cum laude* in 1946.

She attended Columbia University to receive her M.A. in elementary education.

She became an authority in early education and child welfare.

Her interests were Black History and issues of civil rights despair.

Her heroines were Harriet Tubman and Susan B. Anthony.

Shirley became increasingly involved in the community,

And had an interest to forge change.

For the people, she was determined to make things better within her range.

She entered politics and remained accountable to the people and not the party.

She was elected to the New York State Assembly in 1964

After campaigning without the support of the Democratic party.

She was the first Black woman to hold that position.

During her four years, in the statehouse,

Nine of her bills passed by the assembly and four were signed into law,

To better the plight of the people, they passed all without a flaw.

In 1968 she ran as a Democratic candidate for Congress,

Continuing to surrender to the wishes of the people, correcting wrongness.

She was elected to the 91st Congress from Brooklyn.

The first Black woman to serve in the legislative body.

After the 1970 re-election she declared herself:

A candidate for president of the United States.

She declared that she ran for president",

To crack the ice a little more despite the hopeless odds,

To demonstrate the sheer will and refusal to accept the status quo"!

After a successful 14-year Congressional career,

She returned to what she held dear.

In 1983 she returned to education to support great minds to adhere.

She taught at Mt. Holyoke College in Massachusetts.

She felt that her run for president opened the doors,

For children of color and Blacks to run also because she had dared to.

Shirley Chisholm and Rosa Park

Althea Gibson (1927-2003)

Althea Neale Gibson was born on August 25, in Clarendon County, a town

called Silver.

She was the daughter of sharecroppers, so it was told.

They would seek a better life and try hard to be bold.

They took up roots trying to be bold.

The family moved to Harlem, New York when Althea was three years old.

They were not looking for fame, and fortune, or to become wealthy.

She disliked attending school so much that she often played hooky.

Althea spent her early years cutting school and playing sports.

She stated that her daddy whipped her, but she did not blame him.

She said that she deserved it. She just adored being on the courts.

Aside from an occasional fight, she was never in any real trouble.

What Althea liked to do was play sports, at first, basketball was her favorite.

She became proficient in paddle tennis. In sports, she was deeply passionate.

A gracious musician offered her a tennis racket, and she immediately took

to the game. She was good at it and she was instantaneously hooked.

She excelled at paddle tennis and caught the attention of Buddy Walker,

a Police Athletic League supervisor, who suggested she try regular tennis.

Walker took Althea to do training at the Harlem River Tennis Courts.

Within days smashing local male players, against her they were worthless.

She suspended high school because she could not stand classes. She began

competing in girls' tournaments under the almost all black sponsorships of the

American Tennis Association. They were no match, and she was riveting.

In 1946, she attracted the attention of a couple of tennis playing doctors,

Hubert Eaton of North Carolina and Robert W. Johnson of Virginia,

who were active in the black tennis population.

For her natural abilities they had great admiration.

Sugar Ray Robinson and his wife had befriended Althea and advised with cheer

to go South. Each doctor took her into his family. Eaton during the school year,

Johnson in the summer to provide tennis training and to get her on the direct

path for her education.

In 1949, in Wilmington, N.C. she reentered high school for her last three years

and graduation.

Althea could play and win major tennis tournaments, but she had another

opponent not on the court which she had less control of to defeat, name

segregation.

Blacks were not permitted to play tennis at the U.S. National Championships.

Cracks soon developed in the lily-white sport. And ultimately, in 1950, when

Althea was 23 years old, she was permitted to play at the U.S. Nationals,

becoming the first Black to compete in the tournament. She also later went on

and cracked the color barrier at Wimbledon.

As the two-time winner of the black women's tennis championship national,

she thought she had a good case for being admitted to the 1950 U.S. Nationals.

But it appeared as if she was going to be shut out again until a magazine reporter

publicly challenged a match against her on the court.

Finally, the U.S. Lawn Tennis Association relinquished, and she was invited.

In her historic first appearance at the 1950 U.S. Nationals, Barbara Knapp,

in straight sets she overpowered.

Her second-round match on the grass of Forest Hills was against

Louise Brough, who had won the previous three Wimbledons.

Althea would be a match for her too when it was all said and done.

After being beaten 6-1 in the first set, Althea recovered to win the second

set 6-3 and led 7-6 in the third when a thunderstorm struck, terminating the

match.

When it continued the next day, Althea dropped three straight games and lost.

The momentum before the thunderstorm, she seemed not to be able to catch.

It took Althea a while to adjust to the stronger competition. She also remained

unwelcome at some clubs where her tournaments were held was taking a strain.

Hotels would not provide her a room, and even one where she was being

honored.

Even though she was ranked No. 9 among American women in 1952,

It wasn't until four years later that she displayed the game of a player

first level ready to move into.

She preferred to play an attacking game. Being an athletic woman,

she had good foot velocity, allowing her to take control of the court.

As she grew older, she became more consistent from the baseline.

There were no professional tennis tours in those days.

She played a series of matches before Harlem Globetrotter basketball games.

She turned to the pro golf tour for a few years, but she did not become famous.

She tried playing a few events after open tennis started in 1968.

By then she was in her 40s and too old to defeat her younger opponents.

She worked as a pro tennis instructor after she stopped competing.

She coached until 1992 when she retired.

Althea turned into a loner in her well-kept garden apartment in East Orange, N.J.

She was suffering in silence from a series of strokes and ailments brought on by a "terminal." Disease.

After several years of declining health, she died on September 28, 2003, at Orange East General Hospital in East Orange, NJ.

She built on a legacy for those that were before her like Lucy Diggs Slowe, Ora Washington, and Arvelia Myers and left one for other current well-known players such as Serena and Venus Williams, Sloane Stephens, Madison Keys, and Coco Gauff to follow

<u>Quotes:</u>

"No matter what accomplishments you make, somebody helped you."

"I don't want to be put on a pedestal. I just want to be reasonably successful and live a normal life with all the conveniences to make it so."

"In the field of sports, you are more or less accepted for what you do rather than what you are."

Althea Gibson

https://www.loc.gov/item/95512217/

Lorraine Vivian Hansberry
(1930-1965)

Lorraine Hansberry was born in Chicago on May 19, 1930.

Her father was a prosperous entrepreneur.

He and his wife relocated from the South to Chicago,

Trying to have a better life for their family, from their old home they had to go.

Life in Chicago was promising to be more productive.

However, when he bought a home in an all-white community,

Racist backed by the Illinois laws protested and eventually,

The family was forced to move.

He took it to the Supreme court and won.

However, the ordeal took a financial and psychological toll when it all was done.

In 1945 he died of cerebral hemorrhage.

His plan of moving to Mexico ended.

This ordeal influenced Lorraine greatly.

Later, she would write a play using many of the experiences.

She attended Chicago public schools and was an avid reader.

She later attended the University of Wisconsin studying stage design and art.

She realized her love for the stage while at Wisconsin.

Following the location of her interest, in 1950 she went to New York.

In 1951 while working as a waiter, she met the owner's son.

They got married. She busied herself writing short stories, poetry and plays,

For pieces later awards would be won.

Between 1956 and 1957 she dedicated her time to writing "A Raisin in The Sun".

A lot of the experiences of her childhood,

Her family's experience in the White neighborhood,

Their great effort to keep their home was the main plot.

They still lost their home after all was fought.

The success was immediate upon the play's debut on March 11, 1959.

The overwhelmingly acceptance of the play was a good sign.

The play had a 19-month run and won the author the coveted Drama Circle Award. The play was later adopted into a movie.

The popularity of the play and movie were depicting the housing injustice,

She and her family faced were a delayed reward.

In 1963 cancer struck Patricia and she was frequently in the hospital Until her death in 1965. Determined to continue writing,

She wrote her second Broadway play that opened October 1964.

Three months before she died.

Her true abilities will never be known except that she opened doors.

For those who came after her and for those there have been,

Very few Broadway playwrights that have preceded her with the color of her skin. As a tribute to her, her husband compiled,

And edited her work of wisdom statements that was published in 1969.

Oprah Gail Winfrey (1954-

Oprah Gail Winfrey was born January 29, 1954.

She is one of the most influential idols that I know.

Born into poverty in rural Mississippi to a single teenage mother.

Mother was a housemaid and father a coal miner,

He was in the military when Oprah was born and later became a barber.

Raised the first six years of her life with the maternal grandmother.

Oprah often wore dresses made of potato sacks.

Other children made fun of her, but she took solace in her raps.

She interviewed her homemade doll and crows sitting on the fence.

Some may have thought that she had no sense.

Her grandmother taught her to read before the age of three.

At the local church, she was nicknamed "The Preacher".

She stood reciting verses from the Bible in front of her

captured audience, much like her doll and crows, as quiet as could be.

Her reading, Bible verse reciting, and her practice doing interviews,

would soon become a source of immeasurable revenue.

Her grandmother's influence encouraged her to speak in public,

Igniting a positive fire and sense of herself that was not unlit.

She later moved in the inner-city of Milwaukee with her mother,

Who was less supportive and encouraging than her grandmother.

She attended <u>Lincoln High School in Milwaukee</u>,

Later, the <u>Upward Bound</u> program early on was a victory.

She was transferred to the affluent suburban <u>Nicolet High School</u>.

Being continually reminded of her poverty,

As she rode the bus, others she wanted to fool.

To keep up with her peers, rebelled and stole money from her mother's purse,

Her mother once again sent her to live with her father as a result.

Although this time, she did not take her back or bother.

Her half-sister was born but later died of <u>cocaine</u> related causes.

Her mother later gave birth to another daughter,

For her fate adoption would <u>betroth her</u>.

She also had a son who died of Aids.

Oprah was <u>molested</u> by her cousin, uncle, and a family friend,

Starting when she was not even at the age of ten;

For her there was no one to defend.

At age 24, she revealed the abuse with family members to no positive end,

They would not believe her, try to comprehend, or help her to mend.

Not believing in her only gave the perpetrators endorsement for offensives past,

And most likely giving them approval to other to do it again.

At 13, after enduring abuse for years, Oprah ran away from home.

She became pregnant at the age of fourteen.

Her son was born <u>too early</u> and died in infancy;

Not much more than a baby herself scarcely.

But her experience openly discussed on her TV show regarding sexual <u>abuse</u> was

truly heard and believed by her fans including this author.

We did not feel isolated and like a victim anymore.

To help save them, we could share with our sons and daughters.

We were living in silence and not being believed as well.

Nonetheless, being open helped more people world over than anyone can tell.

Her first job as a teenager was working at a local grocery store.

Her father was strict but encouraging, for her there would be so much more.

He made her education a priority, never accepting anything less.

Oprah became an honors student, and was voted Most Popular Girl,

She joined her high school speech team placing second in the nation,

In dramatic interpretation, at the age of 17, Oprah won the Miss Black Tennessee

beauty pageant.

She also attracted the attention of the local black radio station;

While still in high school, she landed a job in radio demonstrating actively.

Extraordinary talents for things to come the whole world would see.

With this foundation, by age nineteen, she was a co-anchor,

Delivering the local evening news with emotions and with spontaneity.

Soon becoming the first black female news anchor,

Leading her to her career in the daytime talk show arena.

She worked there during her senior year of high school,

And first two years of college. She had won an eloquence contest,

Securing her a full scholarship to <u>Tennessee State University</u>,

Studying <u>communication</u>. She did not submit her final paper,

Causing her to receive her degree in 1987,

At which time she was already a successful television celebrity.

Within months after Oprah took over a talk show, it went from last place,

to ratings the highest-rated talk show in Chicago.

She had moved a third-rated local Chicago talk show to first place.

She soon launched her own production company for her base,

becoming an American talk show host, television producer,

Actress, author, <u>humanitarian</u>, and helping others to be achievers.

Oprah swiftly rose to host the most popular talk show on TV in a field,

dominated by white males caught them by surprise and spent their wheels.

Other talk show interviewers standing up to her were no match.

Her rise in popularity and influence on her viewers they could not catch.

Becoming well-known because of her genuine compassion for humanity,

her show was the highest-rated television program of its kind in history.

From 2004 to 2006, she was the world's only Black billionaire.

In 2003, the first Black woman in the world that achieved status of billionaire,

listed as both the most influential woman;

and the most influential Black person of her generation.

She has been noted as "America's most powerful woman.

She has a loyal following; credibility; talent; and doing it all on her own,

No inheritance, favors, gifts, assistance from other, or loans.

Oprah became wealthy and more powerful beyond anyone wildest imagination.

She is one of the most admired women in the world, not just this nation.

As a political force in the 2008 presidential race of Barack Obama,

her endorsement estimated to be worth one million votes.

With a twenty-five-year run and national syndication earned her the title,

the ***"Queen of All Media,"*** and she became the richest Black woman, on air.

She was the 20th Century and North America's first Black <u>multi-billionaire</u>.

Her <u>humanitarian</u>, caring, and compassionate nature most do not share.

Oprah has been ranked the greatest Black philanthropist in American history.

She was ranked as the most influential woman in the world and

shares her story. Oprah later founded her own successful network.

She always does her best work.

Oprah is known as the richest self-made woman in America.

She has the ***"Midas Touch"*** , Everything she touch, turns to gold!

In 2015, Oprah purchased a minority stake in Weight Watchers

for $34 million. By 2020, the value of her shares had soared to as much as $430

million. She also is a shareholder in True Food Kitchen.

She owns a 42-acre estate in California with ocean and mountain view haven

retreats in New Jersey; an apartment in Chicago; an estate in Florida; a ski house

in Colorado; and properties on Maui, Hawaii, Antigua, and in Washington

State. She has ownership of properties not in just this nation.

Oprah has received many awards and recognitions.

In 1989, she was accepted into the NAACP Image Award Hall of Fame.

She was awarded the Spingarn Medal from the same.

President Barack Obama bestowed upon her the Presidential Medal of Freedom.

She was also selected as a member of the American Academy of Arts and Science.

Oprah has received countless awards and honors.

She also received honorary degrees from Duke and Harvard.

She was inducted into the <u>National Women's Hall of Fame</u>;

Received eighteen <u>Daytime Emmy Awards</u>; the Lifetime Achievement Award;

The Chairman's Award; two <u>Primetime Emmy Awards</u>;

the Bob Hope Humanitarian; A <u>Tony Award</u>; a <u>Peabody Award</u>;

and the <u>Jean Hersholt Humanitarian Award</u>;

Oprah was awarded by the <u>Academy Awards</u>; and two additional Academy Award nominations.

Oprah is caring, willing to help other to succeed, empathetic, and generous.

In 2018, Winfrey donated $500,000 to the March for Our Lives student demonstration in favor of gun regulation in the United States.

She has given away more than $400 million to educational causes.

In 2012, Oprah had given over 400 scholarships to Morehouse College in Atlanta, Georgia and many other places not worried about filling her wallet.

After two decades on national TV, to thank her workers and to celebrate, their hard work, she took her staff and their families, in total over one thousand people, employees and families, all together, not to alternate. A vacation to Hawaii, a dream vacation to enjoy and rejuvenate. Their work already good would only escalate.

In 1998, she created the Oprah's Angel Network, a charity that supported projects that were charitable.

Nonprofit organizations grants she provided world over were receivable. In the wake of Hurricane Katrina, Oprah formed the Oprah Angel Network Katrina Registry which raised more than $11 million for relief efforts. Oprah personally gave $10 million to the cause.

Homes were built in Texas, Mississippi, Louisiana, and Alabama. It provided home to the homeless before the one-year anniversary, of Rita and Hurricanes Katrina. She investing $40 million and some of her time to established the Oprah Winfrey Leadership Academy for Girls in South Africa. The school opened in January 2007 on 22 acres.

With an enrollment of 150 students; Later increasing to 450 takers; and contained state-of-the-art classrooms, computer, science laboratories, a library, theatre, and beauty salon.

There have not been any students known to have withdrawn.

Oprah teaches a class at the academy via satellite.

In 2013, Oprah donated $12 million to the Smithsonian's National Museum of African American History and Culture.

Oprah's generosity, openness, compassion, business savvy, and giving of herself, while continuing to keep her head on her shoulders, with a down-to-Earth manner matches no other.

Kamala Harris, Madam Vice President (1964 -

The formation of Kamala's character was shaped by discussions,

Heard regularly by her grandfather like percussions,

Having a long impact on her hearing him talk politics.

Discussing equal rights, corruption sometimes seemed like a bag of tricks.

Later her passionate conversations with him,

Discussing democracy impacted her political career as well,

Not being a whim.

Her grandfather worked for the Indian government,

Defying the conservative label as his foundation.

He worked for historic change and served for years,

After independence as a stenographer

For the British government and civil servant,

While instilling confidence in women in the family

And was fantastically fervent.

He had a progressive outlook especially when it came

To the education and supporting women.

He believed that sons and daughters should

Be equally educated was his vision.

Harris's mother came to America at the age of 19 to attend UC Berkeley,

And would become a breast cancer researcher.

Indians lived in America, but she did not have many Indian friends.

Her friends and neighbors were Black where she would blend in.

Berkeley being politically motivated,

She found herself quickly in civil rights

Marches and protests that were related.

She soon met Donald Harris a radiate student from Jamaica,

Specializing in leftist economic theory.

Their fight continued and did not grow weary.

They married and had two daughters.

Kamala's mother filed for divorce when she was seven.

After the divorce she remained close to her mother's side of the family.

Kamala was age 12 when her mom, sister, and she relocated in Canada.

Harris soon became constantly active excelling in everything she did.

She also worked on the yearbook and in dance.

Kamala had more of an understanding

Of her Indian heritage as a woman,

Because of her Indian born mother, grandfather, and other supportive,

Indian born family than that of her Black heritage,

Giving her knowledge and inspiration

In her self-confidence that was not distortive.

Her Black culture and legacy however, not much of an importance.

Kamala longed to go back home to America.

She and a friend felt that they did not fit into either,

White" or "Black" groups in Canada being biracial.

They made themselves fit into both in high school like a geyser.

Finally, when she was able to go back to America,

She attended Howard University.

She steered clear of radicalism in her college years,

Choosing to work within the system and pursue pragmatic solutions.

She was a leader that wanted to have an impact,

From issues she worked on known to not turn back.

When she wanted to do something that

She felt was right, her focus was kept intact.

At Howard she earned a reputation in the gathering place.

Students would debate with dignity and grace,

Topics of the time and the school's complicated,

Relationship with President Reagan among some they concentrated.

She was spirited, demonstrated a level of enthusiasm,

A level of preparation that was uncommon and with dynamism.

When she decided to join Alpha Kappa Alpha Sorority,

Harris was more than welcomed.

She stood out, among the popular and stand-out students.

She was popular at the university and always for humanity,

In a nonviolent manner, took on the leading role, taking a stand,

For what she believed in, never placing her head in the sand.

Settling into her pragmatic politics that defined her career,

Felt that Howard was a place that shaped her and eternally held it dear.

Harris encouraged students to get involved,

"If we're going to make progress anywhere, we need you everywhere.

The reality on most matters, somebody is to make a decision, so why not let it

be you."

The win of Vice President moved many Americans to tears for the history made.

Finally, another ceiling shattered for your kids and mine,

The possibilities of a new America when women,

Even a daughter of Jamaican and Indian Immigrants

A Black woman, and a woman of Asian descent,

Could at long last become Vice President,

The second highest position in the land of the free.

Since the formation of the country, not common,

Kamala Harris, the first woman,

Holds the office of Vice President for the whole world to see.

Michelle LaVaughn Obama (1964 -

Michelle LaVaughn Robinson skipped 2nd grade,

She joined a gifted class at Bryn Mawr Elementary School

(Later renamed, Bouchet Academy).

She attended Whitney Young High School,

Chicago's first magnet high school,

Following her resolve to follow her own rule.

Her round trip took three hours.

Hard work and determination would later prove to be of tremendous powers.

Her father was a pump operator for the Chicago Water Department,

Suffering from multiple sclerosis which had a deep-rooted,

And passionate effect on her during her childhood.

Witnessing him not giving in to adversities,

Instead, used two canes to get to his job,

to save money to send her to college.

He was determined to bring her higher.

She decided to use her experiences for "good".

She learned that "the only limit to the height of your achievements,

Is the reach of your dreams and your willingness to work hard for them".

For her father, her alliance with herself was to be determined,

To be a good student and not get into trouble,

Which she turned out to be a gem.

Her mother stayed at home to care for her and her older brother,

Not well known for people of color, until, she entered high school.

Her prudent seeking of knowledge proved

To be a jewel regardless of any discernment.

In college she experienced economic, gender, and racial discrimination.

She earned her bachelor's degree from Princeton University,

And doctor degree from Harvard Law School.

Later, while practicing as an attorney in Chicago,

She met Barack Obama.

They fell in love and were married.

He could not let her go!

In Chicago's City Hall, she worked as an assistant commissioner,

Of planning and development, before,

becoming the founding Executive director

Of the Chicago chapter of Public Allies,

Preparing young people for public service intelligence.

In 1996, she joined the University of Chicago,

As associate dean of student services ready to go.

She developed the university's first community service program.

In 2002, she went to work for the University of Chicago Medical Center.

The vice president of community and external affairs,

In 2005 she would enter.

During these years, the Obamas' daughters Malia and Sasha were born.

Their confirming focus never to turn.

Barack Obama became the first Black president,

The 44th president of the United States for two terms.

Michelle becoming the first Black first lady

Of the United States from 2009 to 2017,

The likes of which had not even been seen on the movie screens.

During Barack Obama's second term, Michelle spearheaded,

The Reach Higher Initiative to help students,

Understand job opportunities clearheaded,

The education and skills they needed for those jobs.

She encouraged young people to continue their education past high school,

In technical schools and community colleges,

As well as at colleges and universities,

To succeed these would be their fuel.

Worldwide, she championed the education of girls and women,

Serving as a role model for women and worked

As an advocate for the awareness of poverty,

Physical activity, education, nutrition, and eating healthy.

Her four main initiatives while in the White House

Became a role model for girls and women.

As an advocate for healthy families,

an advocate for service members and their families,

Higher education, and international adolescent girls' education for a better life

lived happily.

She supported American designers and was considered a moderate priced

fashion icon. Demonstrating to girls and women reasonable fashions Everyone

could afford.

In a commencement address at the City College of New York, She told graduates,

"Never view your challenges as obstacles."

It is a lesson she has embodied all her life.

As a child watching her father, it was her life's strife.

A pump operators' daughter, who rose above and became,

A woman whose influence remains of high ranks,

Michelle continues to be an outstanding motivational,

And Inspirational author,

Quoter of motivation and inspiration quotes for girls and women,

A lawyer and even first Black First Lady of the United States of America.

In 2020, Michelle Obama topped Gallup's poll,

Of the most admired woman in America for the third year running.

Dr. Nancy Diane Young (1969 -

Dr. Nancy Young was born Dec 1,1969 in Los Angeles, California.

She was raised in Compton with siblings, step, and half until age thirteen.

Nancy is the second to oldest of 5 children.

Her mother grew up in Watts, CA and Father in Crewe, Virginia.

Nancy's father was a police and firefighter in the 1950s.

He was a firefighter on an all-Black Crew in Washington DC.

He later became an aeronautical engineer after attending Howard University,

at McDonald Douglas he became the first Black manager.

Her mother worked in documents for LA Times more than 10 years.

She went back to school to obtain her AA, BA, and MBA in Child Development.

Afterwards she opened an in-home daycare which grew to owning a private

school for ages 6 weeks old to 6th grade.

The family lived in Compton until drive-by incidents

started on their street in Sept. nineteen -hundred eighty-two.

A new place in San Fernando in March 1983 was the results of their pursue.

Nancy worked as a babysitter while in elementary school.

She started a nursery at her church.

In 7th through 9th grade, she volunteered at her grandfather's nursing home.

From 10th-12th grade she worked at McDonald's also.

When she graduated from high school, she was accepted by all 6 schools around the country in which she had applied to on full academic scholarships,

Syracuse, University of NY at Buffalo, University of Colorado at Boulder, University

of Oklahoma at Tulsa, UCLA, and UC Berkeley. Syracuse was her choice university, with the goal of becoming an anchor woman in broadcast.

The desire was prevented when her sister became pregnant. She affectionately, being the close-knit family and loving sister, she was willing to make do, and changed to UC Berkeley so she could help her sister raise her nephew.

Nancy learned that change is good for growth. The change from Compton to San Fernando took her from an almost 99% Black school to 1-2% Black school with her being the only Black in almost all her junior high classes. High school was not much different when it came to those in her honor classes.

She ran into overt racism in junior high, but mostly from mean girls because of her intelligence. To their racism she did not listen.

In her education and meeting her goal, she was driven.

She was heard for her ideas and soon found her voice.

This really began her political journey that was her choice.

She graduated from San Fernando High in 1987.

Nancy lived in Oakland for the most part of her college years.

When she started college, she worked for the State Health Department.

She was thrown in a new world of international encounters moving to Berkeley.

She lived in a triple dorm room with one White girl and one Asian girl.

The two roommates were heavy metal lovers. . crazy!

Berkeley was interesting. She had out-of-the box thinking teachers,

Although others were male chauvinist... only appreciated the voice of white males. However, Berkeley's teachers and students were rich in many cultures.

After graduation she worked many places as the only female and for most of the times as the only Black. She found that if she articulated well,

treat everyone with kindness, it would win over the people who would be relevant.

They would later in her political life turn out to be in abundant.

When she graduated from UC Berkeley, she accepted an office manager position in Emeryville, California from 1987-1991.

After getting married in 1992 she moved to Fremont, California.

Starting a church there she helped to run a ministry with her husband.

She is the mother of four children, 3 sons and 1 daughter, all born in Fremont.

They lived there until they moved to Tracy in 2006 for a home they could afford.

She soon became involved in the community that she adored.

Nancy obtained a bachelor's degree in Mass Communications from UC Berkeley.

Less than 1% Blacks were in that major. Her focus was on Broadcast Journalism.

She received a Master's in Business Administration from the University of Phoenix.

In 1994 she went back to college full time at University of Phoenix, San Jose campus, while managing vendor contacts for Lam Research full time plus she went through 2 pregnancies over that two- and one-half years.

She was Class Rep and still graduated in 1996 with 3.8 of the 5% of the class for MBA.

In 2014 she went back to school for her Doctorate in Theology at Good News Seminary. She graduated Salutatorian in 2016, received a Doctorate in Theology. from Good News Seminary and Bible College, a Minister's License from

Pentecostal Assemblies of the World, and Ordination as Pastor from Shield of

Faith International.

Nancy has been active in her community since she was young.

She has authored seven published books.

From the early 1980s, she began mentoring and tutoring,

as well as volunteering at senior homes. She founded His Image

Fremont Youth Group and Women of Integrity. Later she started to mentor in

2006 with her husband, James.

She became vested and involved in her community, bringing transparency,

integrity, and personal investment, actively working to make Tracy in coherency.

Dr. Nancy Young was elected as Mayor of Tracy, California in November 2020!

"Piercing that ceiling, opening the door wider," for young girls and women to

also go through, being the First Black and First Female elected as Mayor of Tracy

in the 21st Century. When she first showed interest in politics in Tracy she was

met with skepticism. People told her to quit, she was wasting her time.

Others told her she was a BAT. . Bay Area Transplant who wanted to make Tracy

like big urban cities. Many came to change their mind about her.

In 2012 starting to serve in the council, she was the second Black person to do

so. She was the city's first Black vice mayor also.

After serving 8 years as Tracy City Council Member, Nancy was elected as mayor.

Nancy had been active in her community since her youth, helping provide real

solutions to real issues and won the job as Mayor with hard work and prayer.

Her focus and aim now are to help foster a city-wide team attitude with "TEAM

TRACY!" Believing that every voice matter, she wants and welcomes input.

She wants the council, staff, and community to work together for a better

outlook.

She believes that all are pieces to the puzzle that needs to be able to articulate.

Bringing all the voices together she feels is her job, not to manipulate.

Her commitment is to preserve the city's family-oriented community, accentuate common goals between people; help others achieve growth, and deliverance in their lives through mentorship and ministry.

Nancy believes that strong families make a strong community.

Nancy is committed to continuing effective, experienced, and seasoned leadership.

She is ready to demonstrate to the citizens that these qualities she has ownership.

As mayor, she is ready to address what the residents want and need.

Fulfilling promises and integrating the voice of every citizen she plans to heed.

She "always came to the city council meetings prepared with two things: enough information to form an opinion and enough openness to change her mind."

She continues to be one of the best compassionate and caring people you can find. Nancy is more than good ideas and intentions. As city council for eight years and Vice Mayor, she has a proven and effective record that she left behind.

Rachel Meghan Markle (1981 -

Meghan was born in Los Angeles on August 4, 1981.

Her white American father worked as a director of photography

And lighting for a well-liked TV series that Meghan and her paternal

Half-siblings would go to visit frequently.

She grew up in Los Angeles attending Hollywood Little Red Schoolhouse.

Megan identifies as being mixed-race having a sense of her difference.

At age 11, she communicated to Procter & Gamble to create sexual neutral

characteristics for a dishwashing soap commercial that was on television national.

At a young age she recognized that everyone should have recognition.

She was not afraid to speak out to be sure that everyone was represented,

Not just those in media she wanted to portray in the encircle.

Three months afterwards, P&G changed the commercial.

She was raised as a Protestant but she graduated from Immaculate Heart High

School, an all-girl Catholic school.

In 1999, Meghan was accepted to Northwestern University in Evanston, Illinois.

She joined Kappa Kappa Gamma sorority to enjoy.

She had a struggle to get the money together for her tuition.

Relying in part on a loan her father took out and money from her mother,

To pay for these she had to make some decisions.

She accepted a work-study program for income working on campus after class

utilizing it directly to supplement and lower her tuition.

Meghan also received scholarships for academic achievement.

reducing the payable tuition fees was the agreement.

After her junior year, she interned at the American embassy in Buenos Aires,

She soon became well admired.

She had contemplated a political career but did not score high enough, in the

Foreign Service Officer Test to proceed further.

She returned to Northwestern University,

Also attending a overseas study program in Madrid.

In 2003, Meghan earned her bachelor's degree with a double major

in theater and international studies from Northwestern's

School of Communication for her labor.

Meghan is an expert calligrapher and taught classes through her part-time job at

Paper Source, in Beverley Hills, from 2004 to 2005.

She hosted a group of clients teaching them how to do calligraphy.

She would instruct the two-hour classes ambitiously.

In Meghan's early acting career she had some difficulty getting roles due to her

race, not black enough for the black roles, and not white enough for the white

ones. She took on freelance calligrapher to support herself between acting jobs.

She taught bookbinding, acted as a blogger, charity ambassador,

an internship at the U.S. Embassy, and was an advocate.

Her uncle, a retired diplomat helped her a little at age 20 to secure the U.S.

Embassy position with his assistance she would procure.

Little did we know that soon she would be representing actively the first

American and first Black duchess in the royal family.

Her first on-screen appearance was a small role as a nurse in an episode of a daytime soap opera to keep money in her purse.

Meghan also had small guest roles on some television shows.

She appeared in a Fox's series; did several contracts acting and modeling jobs; she appeared in small movie roles; and worked on a game show.

During a time, she lived for nine months each year in Toronto.

She and an American film producer began dating in 2004.

They were married in Ocho Rios, Jamaica on September 10, 2011.

They decided on a no-fault divorce in August 2013.

In June 2016, Meghan began a relationship with Prince Harry,

The son of Princess Diana, a grandson of Queen Elizabeth II.

She had a comfortable friendship with Princess Eugenie, Harry's first cousin and daughter of Prince Andrew before she met Harry.

In November, the prince directed his communications secretary to release a statement on his behalf to express personal concern about derogatory and false comments made about his girlfriend.

In September 2017, Meghan and Prince Harry first appeared together in public.

Harry proposed on one knee while they were roasting chicken.

He had created Meghan's engagement ring that was yellow golden because that is her favorite and the diamonds on either side were from his mother's jewelry that he gave her with pride.

He felt that it was so important for him to know that his mother was with them together and was a part of his journey with his bride.

Historically Royals were required to ask the monarch's permission to marry according to the Royal Marriages Act 1772. Reforms passed by Parliament in

2013 relaxed the rule to marry, but for the next six in line to the throne it is still mandatory, to seek the queen's approval, which also includes Harry.

Meghan became the Duchess of Sussex on May19,2018

In St George's Chapel at Windsor Castle in the United Kingdom.

Royals, celebrities, and close friends the guest list entail.

Her mother was the only family guest watching proudly To see and witness her daughter blazed the trails, becoming princess with the title of Princess Henry of Wales.

In January 2020, Meghan and Harry returned to the UK from a vacation in Canada and announced that to step back on duties was their decision.

Their role as senior members of the royal family would be balanced between the United Kingdom and North America.

For Harry and Meghan, they needed for themselves and family some distance.

A statement released by the Palace confirmed that the duke and duchess were to become financial y independent and cease to represent the Queen.

The duchess loves dogs and had two before meeting Harry.

One had to stay in Canada when she moved to Britain.

When they returning to North America, they included a Labrador Pula to the family.

The duchess had also gotten along well with the queen's dogs early in their relationship. Harry noticed that the queen's dogs that had always barked at him, but for Meghan right away, they befriended.

Meghan had issues with shifting gears from the purpose-driven work she was doing during the week about the needs of people to the glitz and glamour of an award show.

The couple divulged in an Oprah interview that the Royal family discussed changing the rules so Archie, their first born, would not be a prince and suggesting his skin color may have been a factor.

Harry and Meghan turned down the royal title Earl of Dumbarton for Archie.

Harry and Meghan have settled into their neighborhood and Harry's new country.

They have created what they feel is a positive new home for them and their children.

Chase Your Dreams

Dr. Minnie L. Ransom

You are inherently intelligent, creative, and cooperative.

Your whole being is qualitative.

You have endurance, natural survival skills with inherited resilience.

You overcome in a day what most in a lifetime will never experience.

It has made you strong even though sometimes it was not fair.

Find your passion, discover a path, set a goal. God will get you there.

Take your position, even create it with no time to spare.

You can become whatever your heart desires!

Do everything and anything that it requires.

Starting with being the best son, brother, father, husband

to create and bond strong families.

Overcome and ignore all conveyed negativities.

"You can't, shouldn't, "You will be like____", or other put-downs,

All are beneath you, so put them in the ground.

Desire to be doctors, lawyers, scientists, authors, poets, educators,

Inventers, president, innovators, or creators.

You can be artists, athletes, actors, or astronauts.

All are possible, but a failure you are not!

Let positivity set your heart on fire!

A setback sends you higher!

Strip away biases and somehow go around to overcome.

Zip through any restrictive barrier.

Let no one make you believe that you are inferior.

Stand up for what is fair and right!

Follow the Golden Rule with all your might.

Treat others as you want to be treated.

Being kind can never be defeated.

Always having empathy, sympathy, and compassion,

For others cannot and never will be old-fashioned.

Follow your dream, no matter what your given passion.

The Author's Story

Dr. Minnie Ransom knows struggles, discrimination, isolation, adversities, and inequities. Most of all she knows the importance of education.

At birth in Texas, she was shifted from paternal family member to paternal family member where she never felt that she fit in. She never remained in one place for long, causing her to change schools, making it difficult to form bonds with other children who often alienated her. She never knew or rarely saw any of her maternal relatives. She didn't grow up with compliments or encouragements for her hard work in school except by her teachers who believed in her, demanded excellence, and gave her the desire and encouragement that took her through those dark days.

She relocated to California at the age of 16. She was sexually abused and abandoned. No one believed her just as the perpetrator said and in reality, that gave him permission to continue his behavior which he most likely had done before and continued until someone believed the victim and stopped him. For those who do not understand, abuse is not something children generally make up and want to talk about. Therefore, when they finally put their trust in you to tell you, you should act. She knows if her children or now her grandchildren would have divulged something like that to her, she would have evolved into a mother- bear! Instead of believing her, she was blamed, said she was lying, and was alienated even further. She learned to be silent, never discussed her past around others or only would speak in general terms concerning it.

She existed in foster homes where she never experienced encouragement there as well and was only subjected to much of the same put downs as in Texas. It seemed that the teachers did not care if she would sink or swim either. Through it all she still managed to graduate from high school a semester ahead of her original class with no one in the audience to celebrate for and with her. She exited the Foster system when she was18 and was on her own.

Even the counselor in high school before graduation had advised her to go to a trade school. She successfully completed the trade school and started working in sales. After about three months, she learned that was not something that she cared to pursue. She had always had the desire to teach others.

Minnie knows the meaning of hard work. As a child, she worked in the fields and as a housemaid in Texas. In California, while in high school and as a young adult, she sold Avon, Princess House, sewed for others, created jewelry, and floral arrangements in which she sold. She started working full time as a teacher's aide with preschoolers in Berkeley where she lived. She pursued her dream by working days there and attended college evenings. She worked and paid her way through college until she received her degree. There were times she would carry a full load of 12 or more units and still managed to make the Dean's list.

She knows discrimination on many levels. As a child during the Summers and Christmas breaks, she endured hard work that only Blacks did. After receiving the hard-earned money, she and her neighbor were only allowed in certain stores and those would not allow them to try on the clothes. She and her neighbor soon started to make their own clothes after taking sewing classes at school.

On rare occasions when she was able to go to the movies with her neighbor, paying her own admission, they would have to go to the balcony through a rear door where Blacks could sit.. The signs were also all over reminding races not to mix such as on drinking fountains, entrances, and bathrooms. They always had to enter through a separate entrance. They had to take long bus rides to school on a bus passing the White schools. Their books were old, but the teachers believed in students learning or not passing. Minnie excelled in academics and her teacher had her moved to an advanced class in the six grade.

In California, often Minnie was the only Black in classes throughout high school and college. There were never any personal connections with her teachers. She just did the required work. When she went to stores, she would be followed around. So, she would just leave. This also helped to develop the attitude that she did not want anything to do with sales in the upscale department store that she was hired to work in after graduating from high school and the Manpower Training Program.

In her personal life, she was once told by an insurance broker that he could not insure her new car she was getting because she might see her x-husband and run him over which never was her intention or had ever entered her thoughts. She had just exited a very short marriage and was getting reestablished on her own. She had allowed him to keep the car that they had bought together if he kept up the payments. She took public transportation and was finally able to purchase her car which she was the first-time owner of. She also was able to secure insurance through her union before taking the car off the car lot.

People have questioned her present husband and her about how they accomplished what they have in negative ways. For example, when they moved to the suburbs, people, complete strangers, would ask how they could afford being the first-time owners of a new house in a new neighborhood. There were very few Blacks in the city, but none in the entire track of homes where they were. Her family was the only one in the entire track of homes for several years. They would be questioned about why and how they were making improvements as they saw them working on their property. They would always imply that they were into something illegal to be able to afford everything. At the store, she had been questioned by complete strangers if her husband was White.

Later when other friends were purchasing custom vans, they purchased their first 19-foot motorhome thinking it was better suited for their family. They were the first owners of it and the subsequent others they would own. In the early 80s, they met some other people out camping and they all decided to form a camping club. Camping together as a club, they would be questioned how they all could afford RVs, if they were celebrities' entourage, had kids in sports, had been in sports etc. They would always imply that their accomplishments were either gotten illegally, were given to them, or were accomplished via sports etc. They would, however, compliment people on their motorhomes, but never asked details or asked any negative probing questions.

Everything was accomplished by God's Grace and Mercy allowing them to work hard and prioritize and without any other support from anyone!

After a nice trip one weekend in their third motorhome, they were almost to their exit for home with their children when several cars pulled up beside them. People in one gave them the finger and from the other, someone threw eggs on their motorhome. They also had eggs thrown on their home once. While looking for a home, they had been taken to the undesirable areas even after telling the realtor where they wanted to look. Minnie had seen some interesting homes driving to and from college she wanted to see. Realtor after realtor would insist that the places they were showing them were all they could afford. Minnie took matters in her own hands and located their future home where they were the first owner of. In her career, after moving to the suburbs because houses that she and her husband liked were not affordable in the Berkeley area, she commuted for two years and could not stand the driving every day, she applied in her city and nearby cities. She was told on several occasions that she was overqualified. She had finished her B.S. degree, had several workshops completed, some extension classes from UC. Berkeley, and had started on her master's degree. While living and working in Berkeley, she had been quickly moved up from teacher's aide to assistant teacher, and to teacher as she completed college work. In less than a year after receiving her degree she was moved up to supervisor.

However, she was never hired for permanent jobs in her new community when she moved from Berkeley. She would only be placed in long-term substituting positions, and regular substituting jobs in her new city.

Usually, when she substituted in the schools there would only be one, if any, Black teacher on the staff at any given school. The teachers she substituted for would request her often and would encourage her to apply for positions that were coming up. She would not get the positions.

She soon became frustrated with this and her husband and she purchased a childcare business that was for sale in her city. Upon meeting the owner, The owner stated that she had never had many Blacks in her school! After acquiring the center, Minnie upgraded the school with computers, new books, fresh paint, and painted murals on the walls, made juvenile bedding and pillows for naptime cots and infant beds, put in juvenile rugs, bought new furniture, and equipment inside and outside, turned the school into an infant care, preschool-3rd grade academic school and childcare program becoming the first Black owned school and childcare in the city as far as she knew.

The student body and staff were always multi-cultural, so the parents, staff, and students voted for "Rainbow School" as the name for the school. She operated the program for 13 years.

While she was the owner/director of the private school, some potential clients would be extremely interested in the program after a conversation with her about the curriculum over the phone. However, when they would arrive, some would direct their greeting to the White employee if in the same room with her and were redirected to her as the director. Sometimes they would say that they had to talk it over with their spouse and of course, they were never heard from again. Then there were others who would enroll and would remain until the school was closed during the economic downfall of the 90s. They also would recommend others to attend the school. The school operated strictly on students' fees and many parents lost their jobs in the Silicon Valley during that time.

Career Day 2003

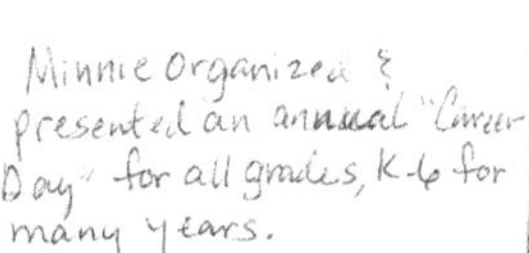

Minnie organized &
presented an annual "Career
Day" for all grades, K-6 for
many years.

ALAMEDA COUNTY OFFICE OF EDUCATION
Curriculum & Instruction

Schooling Language Minority Students
for the Twenty-First Century
A Multidistrict Trainer of Trainers Institute

honors

Minnie Ransom

for Successful Completion of the Year 1 Program

This 23rd day of May, 1996

CHERYL HIGHTOWER
Assistant Superintendent

MARCUS MARTEL
Program Manager

ALAMEDA COUNTY OFFICE OF EDUCATION
Curriculum & Instruction

Schooling Language Minority Students
for the Twenty-First Century
A Multidistrict Trainer of Trainers Institute

honors

Minnie Ransom

for Successful Completion of the Year II Program

This 22nd day of May, 1997

CHERYL HIGHTOWER
Associate Superintendent

MARY-LOUISE NEWLING
Program Director

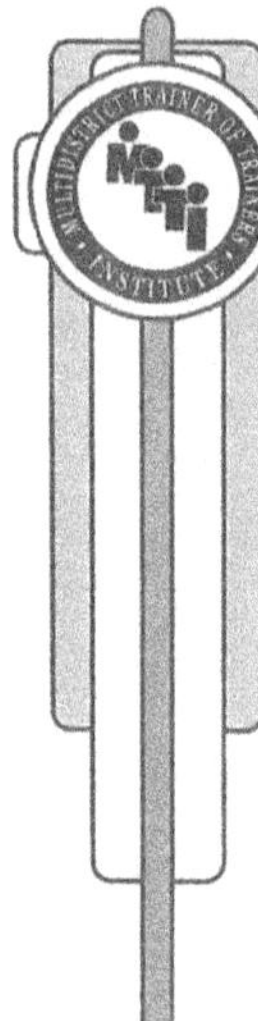

ALAMEDA COUNTY OFFICE OF EDUCATION
Curriculum & Instruction

Schooling Language Minority Students
for the Twenty-First Century
A Multidistrict Trainer of Trainers Institute
honors

Minnie Ransom

for Successful Completion of the Three Year Program

This 22nd day of May, 1998

KAREN MARELLI
Assistant Superintendent

MARY-LOUISE NEWLING
Program Director

A
Miniconference

Language

Students

April 25, 1998

Alameda County Office of Education
313 West Winton Avenue, Hayward, California

Cheryl Hightower, Superintendent

Schooling Language Minority Students

April 25, 1998

Dear Conference Participants:

Welcome to Schooling Language Minority Students for the Twenty-First Century: A Miniconference. This miniconference provides the Year III MTTT graduates an opportunity to showcase their staff development skills and at the same time provide Alameda County educators an opportunity to enhance their repertoire of effective strategies for working with language minority students.

These graduates have completed three years of dedicated study of theory and practical application to prepare them to become outstanding educators and viable staff developers. We will experience the outcome of their commitment to three years of involvement in the Multidistrict Trainer of Trainers Program completed at the Alameda County Office of Education.

This one day miniconference promises to provide a wealth of information and pleasure. Thank you for joining us.

Sincerely,

Mary-Louise Newling, Coordinator
Curriculum & Instruction

PROGRAM
Saturday, April 25, 1998

8:30 - 8:45 Coffee/Registration

8:45 - 9:00   Opening General Session   (Room 142)
Mary-Louise Newling

9:15 - 10:30   Workshops Session I   *(Select One)*
MTTI Year III Graduates

10:45- 12:00   Workshops Session II   *(Select One)*
MTTI Year III Graduates

12:00 - 1:00   LUNCH

                  Storyteller Awele Makeba   *(Room 142)*

1:15 - 2:30   Workshops Session III   *(Select One)*
MTTI Year III Graduates

2:30 - 3:00   Closure   *(Room 142)*

Outcomes

*By the end of the Miniconference, participants will
have:*

◆   *Developed* an understanding of how they can use
a variety of structures, practices, strategies, and
techniques to assist language minority students in
their classrooms and schools.

◆   *Examined* how the culture(s) and language(s) of
language minority students can be used to
enhance their educational experiences.

◆   *Identified* curriculum materials, literature, multimedia
materials, information, ideas, manipulatives, artifacts,
and other resources which they can use to assist
language minority students in their classrooms and
schools.

Session #IIB

Minnie Ransom   Room 213
                                          10:45 - 12:00

Workshop Title:
Strategies To Value Diversity in the Classroom

Participants will:
- Explore strategies for teaching in a diverse classroom and building bridges between cultures.
- Explore strategies which lead to an additive, rather than a subtractive, approach to cultures.
- Engage in real life activities that connect parents to their children's learning.
- Address diverse cognitive styles and multiple intelligences.

About the Presenter:
Minnie Ransom is a classroom teacher with the Fremont Unified School District. She has had a wealth of experience working with adults and students in multicultural and economically diverse populations. She has worked with Berkeley Unified School District as an aide, teacher, and administrator where she developed curriculum for use by staff and parents. She has owned and directed a private school and childcare center. A graduate of California State University, Hayward, Minnie has both Early Childhood and Adult Education credentials.

Certificate
of
Special Recognition

This certifies that

Minnie Ransom

is honored as a

Teacher of the Year Nominee

for exemplary contribution and dedication to the students of the

Fremont Unified School District

Given at _Board of Education Meeting_ _October 13_, 19_99_

Dr. Ransom with Miss Martha Holcombe Root, creator and founder of "All God's Children" dolls that she collects.

Some of the activities from Dr. Ransom's Private school and childcare.

*Some students in the playground at **Rainbow School in Union City, CA** ((Minnie Ransom's private school).*

CONCEPTS WERE INTRODUCED IN A VARIETY OF WAYS.
WINNERS OF EASTER EGG HUNT.

*Minnie **Ransom** and students at **Rainbow School in Union City, CA** (Her private school) celebrating Hawaiian Day one of many cultural events.*

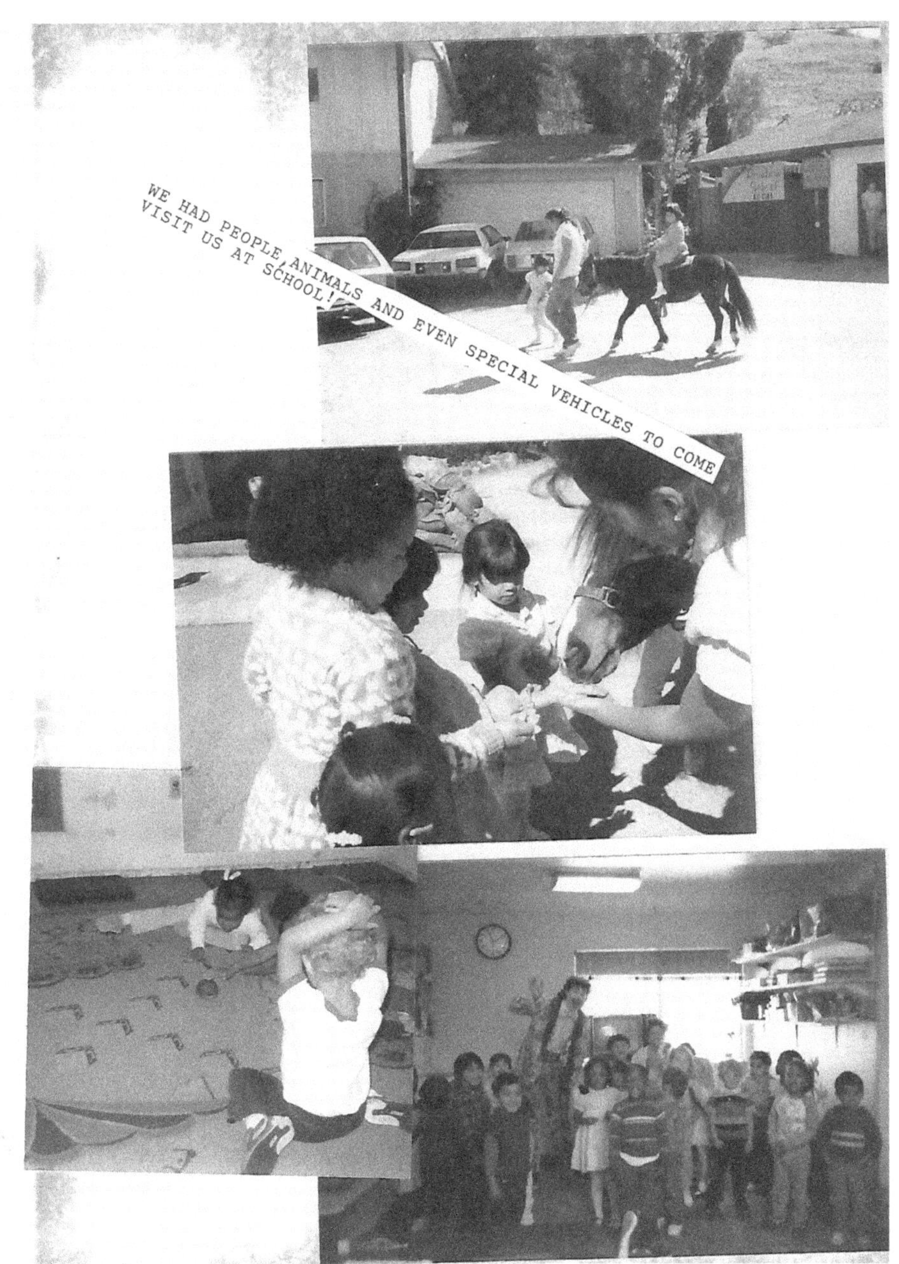
WE HAD PEOPLE, ANIMALS AND EVEN SPECIAL VEHICLES TO COME
VISIT US AT SCHOOL!

UNION CITY POLICE'S TALKING CAR
Our friends the
Deer Family

After applying later in the same nearby school districts and the county office, she had applied previously; she was offered employment in all positions that she applied for. One day before she was to visit a school that she was being offered, she received a phone call to participate in an interview. She decided to participate and she was hired on the spot. She remained at that same district/school until retiring. She was the only permanent Black teacher and/or staff member for 26 years there. She believes from all accounts that she was the first Black teacher there. When she was there, there was a Black custodian for one year and two temporary teachers at different times who each remained one year. At times there she had encountered and endured some staff not speaking or acknowledging her even when she spoke first.

On some occasions the person walking behind her would get acknowledged but not her. It is in her nature to speak, so she continued even when she had decided not, it would come out. Eventually she began to be respected.

During her time with the district/school, she contributed to the school community.

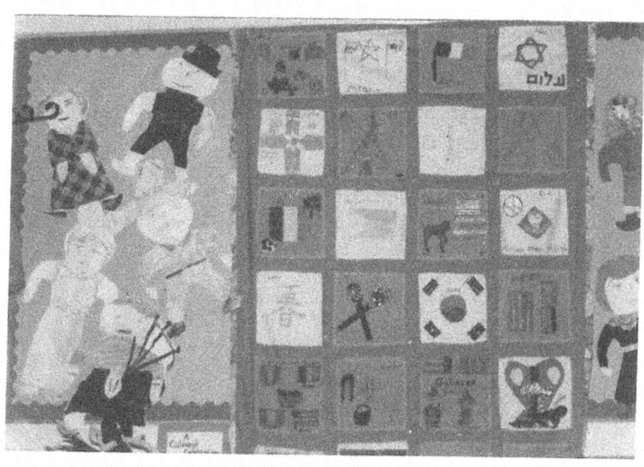

Dr. Ransom not only took many Professional Development classes provided by her district, she also completed programs through the County Superintendent Office of Education and provided workshops there in her desired subject, Multi-Cultural and English Learners.

When her husband retired, she supported him in his sauce and catering business (PJRs Gourmet Sauces and Catering). She obtained appropriate licenses, secured the trademark, developed the label, rewrote his recipe allowing bottlers to create their formula for mass production. She created flyers, and information for the website. She was able to secure his first placement in two supermarket chains.

Later in life, she pursued her education again and received her Master and Ed. D. Degree all while continuing to work full time, be a wife and mother. She has spent her life educating others from teaching her cousins as a child in Texas what she had learned in school to becoming a life-long educator in her private school, a Juvenile facility, adult school, public elementary schools, middle schools, and with her church youth groups. She has also worked to serve the homeless and mentor youth. She serves on the board for at risk students in her city. Inspired by Oprah Winfrey, she had been encouraged to tell her story and not keep feeling like a victim, ashamed, hurt for not being believed, blaming herself for other's actions, and to not feel guilty when others tag her with the blame. She has had a desire to educate in the form of print and this is the adventure in pursuing that dream.

Student's Book Review:

"So far, the book is really interesting. Now I know about Harriet Tubman because of your book. Its good for 4th graders because we need to learn this. I like the book because it is interesting." 5 Star Review***** Omar

"I really loved it and it was very sad and informative." 5 Star Review ***** Razvan

"I really like your book because I liked that you talked about Black women and how they live or died and what they did. Its third/fourth grade level." 5 Star Review*****

"Your book is very detailed and it teaches a lot I didn't know! My class room 13 has started with Harriet Tubman. I am being honest, and I give your book a 5 Star Review *****." You are the best author!!! Go Mrs. Ransom! I encourage you to keep writing!" Mikael

Book Review: 5 Star*****Ryder

"I liked it and it has some things that I never knew about, but overall it is a 5 Star *****." Hareet

"I liked how you used poetry to talk about all the Black women. I want to give this book a 5 Star Review*****."

"Pictures are amazing! I like how she saves people. She is caring. It is so cool to live 93 and to see the Queen! I think it is 3-5th grade level. It would have been better if there were more pictures. But overall I think the story is wonderful. *****

"Informal, amazing, art (illustration), amazing back 5 Stars *****. This book is awesome! 3rd/4th grade level" Murtaza

"I love your drawings. And guess what, I am doing an essay on Harriet Tubman. You gave me so much information but there are some big words so I think it would be for 3rd -6th grade. 5 Stars*****" Sana

"I think we all can make a difference." My rating 5 Stars*****

"It is a 5 Star rating *****but I like Ruby Bridges in the book."

"I love the Font, the details. I love the book. I give it a 5 Star ***** and I think it would be perfect for 4th grade." Arjana

"I like it. I like the cover and its about Black women and I like that because they get treated unfair in the old time. 5 Star*****" Ashleen

"I love learning about Black people and it is a good book. 5 Stars*****

"I rate the book 5 Stars*****. I like your wording. It would probably be more for older kids than younger kids. I want to be an author when I grow up. So I will use your book for help. Thank you. I love your book. Thank you." Mubarlca

"I like the poetry and history. It would be better if you put pictures of the events like the escapes and rescues so 1st and 2nd can read it." 4 Stars **** Noah

"It is a really good book and how it was really detailed. I think the age level is 4th – 6th. My rating about this book 5/5 Stars*****." Faryal

www.ingramcontent.com/pod-product-compliance
Lightning Source LLC
Chambersburg PA
CBHW040805120726
48005CB00012B/1305